101 FUNNY OFFICE PRANKS

GiggleGenius Publishing

© 2024 GiggleGenius Publishing

No part of this book may be reproduced, stored in a retrieval system, or transmitted in any form or by any means (electronic, mechanical, photocopying, recording, or otherwise) without the written permission of the author.

PLAY NICE
A Prankster's Code of Conduct

This book is purely for entertainment and should be enjoyed as such. The author and publisher assume no liability for the antics you choose to perform. Remember, with great pranking comes great responsibility, so always consider the potential outcomes. Approach each prank with kindness and a good-natured spirit, never with malice.
Ready for some fun?
Let's dive in, but let's keep it friendly!

PRANK CHECKLIST

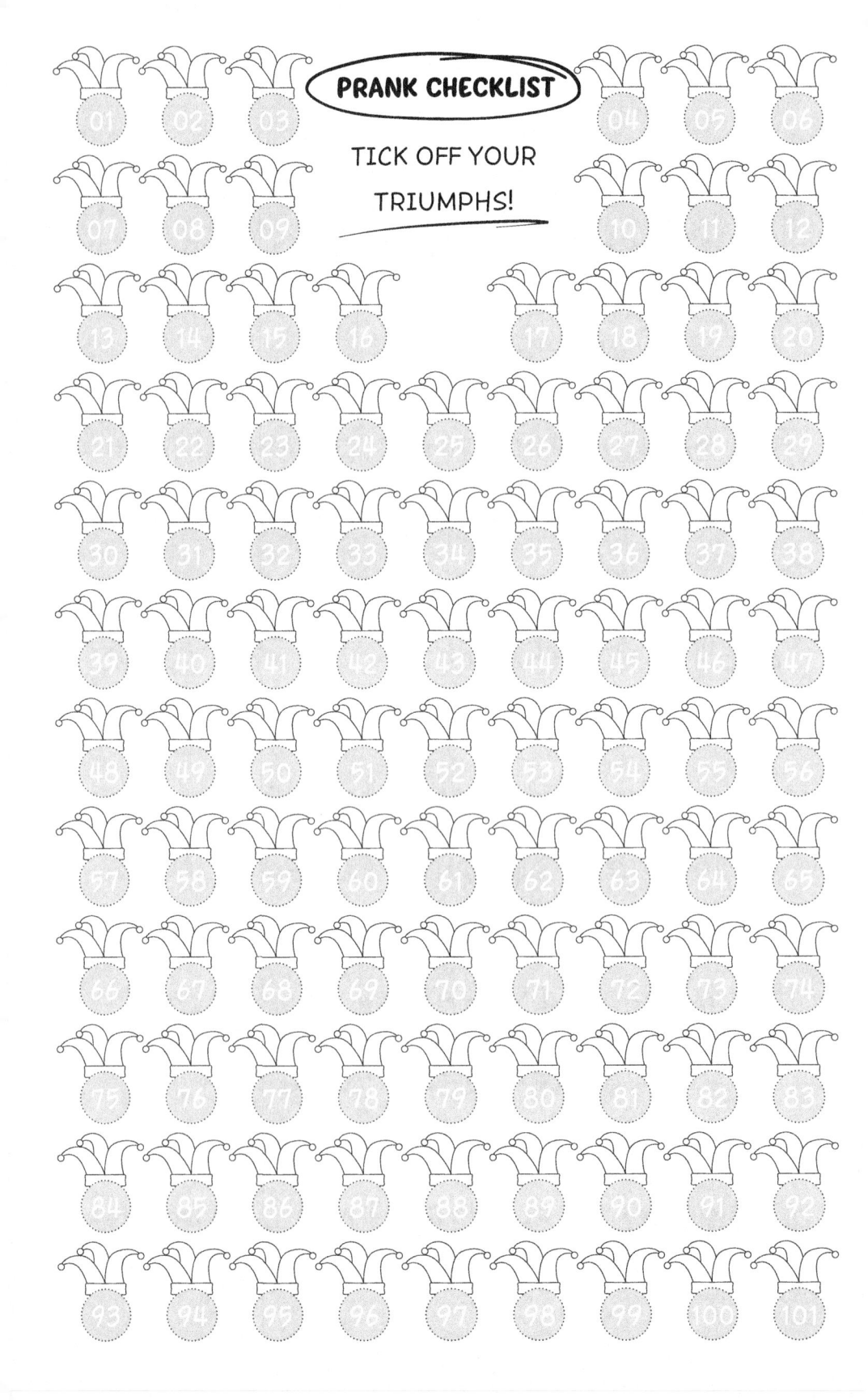

TICK OFF YOUR TRIUMPHS!

01 02 03 04 05 06
07 08 09 10 11 12
13 14 15 16 17 18 19 20
21 22 23 24 25 26 27 28 29
30 31 32 33 34 35 36 37 38
39 40 41 42 43 44 45 46 47
48 49 50 51 52 53 54 55 56
57 58 59 60 61 62 63 64 65
66 67 68 69 70 71 72 73 74
75 76 77 78 79 80 81 82 83
84 85 86 87 88 89 90 91 92
93 94 95 96 97 98 99 100 101

THE MASTER PRANKSTER'S INDEX

#1	JELL-O DESK SURPRISE 01
#2	MOUSE SENSOR MISCHIEF 02
#3	DESK MEADOW PRANK 03
#4	DESKTOP FLIP TRICK 04
#5	KEYBOARD CONFETTI 05
#6	RUBBER BAND BUZZ 06
#7	SCISSORS IN A ZIP TIE 07
#8	CHAIR HORN SURPRISE 08
#9	TOILET PAPER ZIPPER 09
#10	THE PERPETUAL POOPER 10
#11	DOUGHNUT DISGUISE SURPRISE 11
#12	THE TOENAIL TREASURE HUNT 12
#13	THE SPIDER SCARE CUP 13
#14	THE TRASH CORPSE 14
#15	THE URGENT CALLBACK 15
#16	ENDLESS ROLL RUSE 16
#17	THE AQUARIUM 17
#18	CARAMEL ONION DELIGHT 18
#19	SNEAKY SOLE SURPRISE 19
#20	SHADOW BUG SHOCKER 20
#21	THE PHANTOM KEYBOARD 21
#22	THE BALLOON BOOBY TRAP 22
#23	THE BANANA RECEIVER 23
#24	THE SMELLY FINGER 24
#25	CUP LABYRINTH 25
#26	GHOSTS IN THE COPIER 26
#27	THE SLIPPERY DOORKNOB 27
#28	THE PERSISTENT PENNY PLOY 28
#29	ARACHNID IN THE ATTIC 29
#30	GOOGLY-EYED GALLERY 30

THE MASTER PRANKSTER'S INDEX

#31	THE COFFEE BLOCK	31
#32	GHOST MOUSE MAYHEM	32
#33	THE FAKE POO	33
#34	THE WRAP TRAP	34
#35	THE "OUT OF ORDER" MIRROR	35
#36	CREAMY SURPRISE	36
#37	THE LATHERLESS SOAP	37
#38	DESK DRAWER CRITTERS	38
#39	THE MYSTERY MOVE-IN	39
#40	THE UNBIRTHDAY SURPRISE	40
#41	THE TYPIST'S TWISTER	41
#42	THE PHANTOM MEOW	42
#43	THE MYSTERIOUS MEMO MIX-UP	43
#44	THE COPYCAT PAPERCLIP	44
#45	THE SCENTED SEAT	45
#46	THE PHANTOM PRINTOUT	46
#47	THE GREAT COFFEE HUNT	47
#48	I SEE YOU	48
#49	THE PARKING PLOT	49
#50	THE FAUXSTING BOX	50
#51	OFFICE CRIME SCENE	51
#52	THE GHOST DESKTOP	52
#53	THE SCRATCH SCARE	53
#54	THE CHATTY COPIER	54
#55	THE BOTTOMLESS BOX	55
#56	THE NEVER-ENDING DOCUMENT	56
#57	THE UN-CLOSABLE DOOR	57
#58	THE FRIDGE FRIGHT	58
#59	THE LABEL EVERYTHING	59
#60	THE SHATTERED SCREEN	60

THE MASTER PRANKSTER'S INDEX

#61 THE ERRATIC MOUSE 61
#62 MUGSHOT SURPRISES 62
#63 CASH HUNT CLIFFHANGER 63
#64 SCENT OF SURPRISE 64
#65 THE UNSLICEABLE SURPRISE 65
#66 THE DESKTOP MIRAGE 66
#67 THE ENDLESS UPDATE 67
#68 THE TEMPTATION TEST 68
#69 THE GREAT SWEET SWAP 69
#70 STAPLER HOSTAGE HEIST 70
#71 THE OUTLANDISH CLIENT REQUEST 71
#72 EXECUTIVE FACE SWAP 72
#73 THE SILENT TECH TANGO 73
#74 THE UNQUENCHABLE THIRST 74
#75 THE CHATTY FLORA 75
#76 FROZEN BUGS 76
#77 THE DESK DILEMMA 77
#78 THE BACKWARD BUREAU 78
#79 THE UNWRAPPING URGE 79
#80 SOLO COSTUME DAY 80
#81 THE NEVER-RIGHT CHAIR 81
#82 THE PHANTOM BROADCAST 82
#83 THE CHAMELEON COUTURE 83
#84 THE WAITING GAME 84
#85 THE GREAT VANISHING DISPLAY 85
#86 THE SILENT SPEAKER 86
#87 THE SEAT SYMPHONY 87
#88 THE OFFICE GAZETTE 88
#89 THE FAUX MILK MISHAP 89
#90 THE UNEXPECTED WORKDAY 90

THE MASTER PRANKSTER'S INDEX

#91 THE FAUX PARKING TICKET 91
#92 THE WILD CALL 92
#93 THE RESTROOM RUSE 93
#94 THE BOSS'S NUMBER 94
#95 THE WATCHFUL EYE 95
#96 THE TIE-DOWN 96
#97 THE CONFETTI SURPRISE 97
#98 THE INKY PHONE 98
#99 THE INVISIBLE INK FIASCO 99
#100 THE ELEVATOR ESCAPADE 100
#101 THE LEAKY CUP 101

#1 JELL-O DESK SURPRISE

WHAT YOU'LL NEED

Jell-O mix, Coworker's stapler or pen holder, A spoon.

HOW IT'S DONE

Prepare Jell-O and immerse a chosen office item, like a stapler or pen holder, within. Let it set to create a wiggly spectacle. The reveal promises a mix of bewilderment and laughter. "Accidentally" leave a spoon nearby, nudging them towards a giggly excavation.

PRANK EXECUTED?

Date: Victim:

HOW DID IT GO?

Repeat Worthy?

#2 MOUSE SENSOR MISCHIEF

WHAT YOU'LL NEED

Tape or a sticky note, a colleague's mouse

HOW IT'S DONE

Place tape or a sticky note over the bottom sensor of a colleague's mouse. This simple action renders the device seemingly useless, sparking confusion and a mini tech mystery. Observe with amusement as they troubleshoot the unexpected "malfunction. Be prepared to reveal the trick and share a laugh together.

PRANK EXECUTED?

Date: .... Victim: ....

HOW DID IT GO? 😊 😒 😠

Repeat Worthy? 👍 👎

#3 DESK MEADOW PRANK

WHAT YOU'LL NEED

Cat grass seeds, A coworker's keyboard, Water

HOW IT'S DONE

Before a coworker heads off on vacation, stealthily plant cat grass seeds under their keyboard keys. Water them lightly to encourage growth. Upon their return, they're met with a surprising green meadow where their keys once were, transforming their desk into a mini oasis. Prepare for a laughter-filled cleanup, bringing a piece of nature into the office.

PRANK EXECUTED?

Date: Victim:

HOW DID IT GO?

Repeat Worthy?

#4 DESKTOP FLIP TRICK

WHAT YOU'LL NEED

Computer with keyboard, Quick fingers

HOW IT'S DONE

When your coworker is away, press CTRL + ALT + ↓ to turn their desktop upside down, causing a playful stir upon their return. This quick trick leaves them puzzled, facing a topsy-turvy digital world. Observe their bewildered attempts to navigate this new orientation. To revert, simply press CTRL + ALT + ↑.

PRANK EXECUTED?

Date: Victim:

HOW DID IT GO?

Repeat Worthy?

#5 KEYBOARD CONFETTI

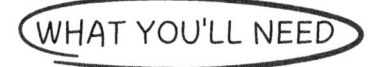

WHAT YOU'LL NEED

coworker's keyboard, Small prying tool. ;

HOW IT'S DONE

Seize a moment when your colleague is away to rearrange the keys on their keyboard using a small tool. This rearrangement turns their typing experience into a perplexing puzzle. Enjoy the confusion as they decipher the new layout. Stand by to help reorder the chaos.

PRANK EXECUTED?

Date: .... Victim: ....

HOW DID IT GO?

Repeat Worthy? 👍👎

#6 RUBBER BAND BUZZ

WHAT YOU'LL NEED

A bunch of rubber bands, Access to a chatty coworker's phone

HOW IT'S DONE

Wrap a talkative coworker's phone in a dense network of rubber bands, creating an amusing barrier. The resulting confusion and attempts to free the phone add a playful challenge to their day. Heighten the amusement by calling their entwined device, inducing a frantic scramble to answer.

PRANK EXECUTED?

Date: Victim:

HOW DID IT GO?

Repeat Worthy?

#7 SCISSORS IN A ZIP TIE LOOP

WHAT YOU'LL NEED

Zip tie, Scissors (to be pranked with)

HOW IT'S DONE

Fasten the scissors' handles with a zip tie, creating a playful puzzle. This jest locks the scissors in a closed position, prompting a humorous quest to solve the paradox without their use. Have a spare pair of scissors ready to resolve the riddle, culminating in shared laughter over the clever setup.

PRANK EXECUTED?

Date: _____ Victim: _____

HOW DID IT GO? 😊 😐 😠

_____
_____
_____
_____

Repeat Worthy? 👍 👎

#8 CHAIR HORN SURPRISE

WHAT YOU'LL NEED

Air horn, Duct tape

HOW IT'S DONE

First, locate a chair commonly used by your colleagues. Position the air horn directly underneath the seat, where it will remain unseen. Carefully use duct tape to secure the air horn in place, ensuring the button is precisely aligned to be pressed when the chair is sat upon. When the victim sits down, their weight triggers the air horn, emitting a loud blast.

PRANK EXECUTED?

Date: _____   Victim: _____

HOW DID IT GO?

Repeat Worthy? 👍👎

#9 TOILET PAPER ZIPPER

WHAT YOU'LL NEED

Zip ties, Toilet paper roll

HOW IT'S DONE

Start by securing a toilet paper roll with several zip ties, tightening them enough to restrict the paper from easily unrolling. Place this modified roll back on the holder in the bathroom. The moment of confusion and slight panic when someone attempts to use it and finds themselves in a bind is where the humor lies. Be ready with a pair of scissors to offer assistance.

PRANK EXECUTED?

Date: Victim:

HOW DID IT GO?

Repeat Worthy?

#10 THE PERPETUAL POOPER

WHAT YOU'LL NEED

A pair of shoes, A set of jeans, Stuffing material (like newspaper or towels)

HOW IT'S DONE

Craft the illusion of an eternal occupant in the restroom using just shoes, jeans, and stuffing. Attach the shoes to the jeans' legs and fill them to appear occupied, positioning them on the toilet seat to simulate someone in endless contemplation. The setup should look as though someone is perpetually in a state of deep reflection on the toilet.

PRANK EXECUTED?

Date: _____ Victim: _____

HOW DID IT GO?

Repeat Worthy? 👍👎

#11 DOUGHNUT DISGUISE SURPRISE

WHAT YOU'LL NEED

Empty doughnut box, Healthy vegetable snacks

HOW IT'S DONE

Start by securing an empty doughnut box, the kind that promises sugary delights within. Instead of filling it with the expected doughnuts, pack it with an assortment of vegetable snacks. Think carrot sticks, celery, or any crunchy vegetables that can masquerade as a disappointment to the unsuspecting sweet tooth. Ensure you have actual doughnuts ready for those craving a genuine sugar hit.

PRANK EXECUTED?

Date: Victim:

HOW DID IT GO?

Repeat Worthy? 👍👎

#12 THE TOENAIL TREASURE HUNT

WHAT YOU'LL NEED

1 iced cake, Green icing

HOW IT'S DONE

Begin with a beautifully iced cake as your canvas. Using green icing, artistically script the message "Find the Toenail" across the top. There are no real toenails lurking in this dessert. The true amusement unfolds as you watch to see who among your peers is brave enough to slice into the cake and debunk the myth of the hidden toenail.

PRANK EXECUTED?

Date: _____ Victim: _____

HOW DID IT GO? 😊 😒 😠

_____
_____
_____
_____

Repeat Worthy? 👍 👎

#13 THE SPIDER SCARE CUP

WHAT YOU'LL NEED

Paper cup, Sticky note, Pen, Small piece of black paper or fabric

HOW IT'S DONE

Write on the sticky note a cautionary message: "WARNING: Huge aggressive spider under cup! DO NOT PICK UP until ready to squish!" Affix this note prominently to the side of the paper cup, then carefully tear a small hole at the bottom of the cup. This suggests the possibility of a spider's escape. Place a tiny piece of black paper or fabric near the hole to enhance the illusion, mimicking a spider lurking nearby.

PRANK EXECUTED?

Date: Victim:

HOW DID IT GO?

Repeat Worthy?

#14 THE TRASH CORPSE

WHAT YOU'LL NEED

Black garbage bags, Tape, Rope or twine

HOW IT'S DONE

Mold garbage bags into a shape that mimics a human body. Use tape to cinch at the 'joints' to give your creation more realistic definition, such as at the 'wrists' and 'ankles,' and use rope or twine to tie off sections to enhance the human form illusion. Once your faux body is assembled, position it beside the dumpster, ideally in a semi-hidden spot where it's not immediately obvious but will eventually be discovered.

PRANK EXECUTED?

Date: Victim:

HOW DID IT GO?

Repeat Worthy?

#15 THE URGENT CALLBACK

WHAT YOU'LL NEED

Sticky note, Pen

HOW IT'S DONE

Jot down "Please call back urgently" on a sticky note, signing off with an indecipherable name. Place it on your chosen colleague or boss's desk. Relish the moment as they embark on a puzzled quest, seeking the mysterious person behind the urgent message.

PRANK EXECUTED?

Date: _____ Victim: _____

HOW DID IT GO?

Repeat Worthy?

#16 ENDLESS ROLL RUSE

WHAT YOU'LL NEED

Duct tape, Toilet paper roll

HOW IT'S DONE

Create the illusion of an infinite toilet paper supply by wrapping a roll entirely in duct tape. It appears usable at a first glance, but the real amusement kicks in when someone attempts to use it, only to realize that it's impossible to peel off even a single sheet. After sharing a laugh, be ready to offer a genuine roll of toilet paper as a friendly resolution to this playful deception.

PRANK EXECUTED?

Date: Victim:

HOW DID IT GO?

Repeat Worthy?

#17 DESKTOP AQUARIUM SURPRISE

WHAT YOU'LL NEED

Clear plastic wrap, Water, Colorful aquarium gravel, Hermit crabs (optional)

HOW IT'S DONE

Convert a desk drawer into a mini aquarium by lining it with plastic wrap and filling it with water. Add colorful gravel for effect, and if you're feeling adventurous, introduce a few hermit crabs. The unsuspecting colleague will be greeted by a lively, aquatic scene upon opening their drawer. Ensure to protect any office supplies from the makeshift tide to keep the surprise purely delightful.

PRANK EXECUTED?

Date: _____ Victim: _____

HOW DID IT GO?

_____
_____
_____
_____

Repeat Worthy? 👍👎

#18 CARAMEL ONION DELIGHT

WHAT YOU'LL NEED

Large onions, Caramel coating, Popsicle sticks, Sprinkles

HOW IT'S DONE

Masquerade peeled onions as caramel apples by dipping them thoroughly into caramel, ensuring a generous layer covers the entire surface. Insert popsicle sticks into their centers and sprinkle them with sprinkles to enhance their visual appeal. Present these faux treats to coworkers and observe their astonishment upon tasting. Cap off the prank by offering genuine caramel apples.

PRANK EXECUTED?

Date: _____   Victim: _____

HOW DID IT GO?

Repeat Worthy? 👍👎

#19 SNEAKY SOLE SURPRISE

WHAT YOU'LL NEED

Googly eyes, Adhesive

HOW IT'S DONE

Quickly attach googly eyes to the front of your colleague's shoes when they're distracted or looking away. Position the eyes just above the toes to ensure they're easily noticed. Use a strong adhesive for a secure fit. After placing the eyes, discreetly step back and blend into your surroundings. Wait for your colleague to notice the quirky addition, leading to a moment of surprise and laughter.

PRANK EXECUTED?

Date: .... Victim: ....

HOW DID IT GO?

Repeat Worthy? 👍👎

#20 SHADOW BUG SHOCKER

WHAT YOU'LL NEED

Black construction paper, Scissors, Tape, A lamp with a lampshade

HOW IT'S DONE

Cut out a bug shape from black construction paper—choose a silhouette that's universally startling, like a beetle, centipede, or spider. Tape your paper bug inside the lampshade of a commonly used lamp. When the lamp is turned on, the "bug's" shadow will be projected, appearing unnervingly large and causing a brief scare among your colleagues.

PRANK EXECUTED?

Date: Victim:

HOW DID IT GO?

Repeat Worthy?

#21 THE PHANTOM KEYBOARD

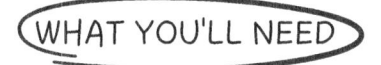

WHAT YOU'LL NEED

Bluetooth keyboard, Optional: Bluetooth mouse

HOW IT'S DONE

Secretly pair the Bluetooth keyboard (and mouse, if you're using one) with your coworker's computer when they're not looking. Once connected, you can type messages or execute commands to create amusing or bewildering moments for them. If you've included a mouse in your prank, you can also move their cursor around to add to the confusion.

PRANK EXECUTED?

Date: _____   Victim: _____

HOW DID IT GO?

Repeat Worthy?

#22 THE BALLOON BOOBY TRAP

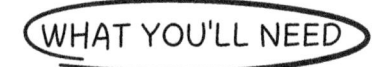

WHAT YOU'LL NEED

Large balloon, Strong tape, Thumbtack or small nail

HOW IT'S DONE

Inflate the balloon and tape the thumbtack (pointy side out) where the door hits it. Position the inflated balloon directly over the tack or nail so that when the door is opened, it presses the balloon against the sharp point. The impact will cause the balloon to burst, creating a sudden loud noise.

PRANK EXECUTED?

Date: Victim:

HOW DID IT GO?

Repeat Worthy? 👍👎

#23 THE BANANA RECEIVER

WHAT YOU'LL NEED

Ripe banana, Coworker's office phone

HOW IT'S DONE

Wait for a moment when your colleague is away from their desk. Quietly remove the handset from their office phone and replace it with a ripe banana, positioning it to mimic the handset's usual placement. Ensure the banana sits naturally. The effectiveness lies in making the setup believable. Upon their return, your colleague will reach for what they think is their phone, only to find the banana in hand.

PRANK EXECUTED?

Date: _____ Victim: _____

HOW DID IT GO?   😊 😐 😠

_____
_____
_____
_____

Repeat Worthy? 👍 👎

#24 THE SMELLY FINGER

WHAT YOU'LL NEED

Onion, garlic, or pickles.

HOW IT'S DONE

Rub office items of your favorite colleague with onion, garlic, or pickles. This could be their pen, hole puncher, or even their mouse – anything they frequently touch. Your colleague will likely be puzzled, wondering where the strange smell on their fingers is coming from as they wash their hands more often.

PRANK EXECUTED?

Date: .... Victim: ....

HOW DID IT GO?

Repeat Worthy? 👍👎

#25 CUP LABYRINTH

WHAT YOU'LL NEED

Many paper cups, water.

HOW IT'S DONE

Fill numerous paper cups with water and arrange them closely together, covering your coworker's desk area completely. This setup creates a challenge where your coworker cannot easily access their desk without removing the cups one by one. Enjoy the spectacle of their careful maneuvering!

PRANK EXECUTED?

Date: _____ Victim: _____

HOW DID IT GO? 😊 😒 😠

_____
_____
_____
_____

Repeat Worthy? 👍 👎

#26 GHOSTS IN THE COPIER

WHAT YOU'LL NEED

A photo of your favorite colleague; photocopier, scissors, (optional) printer.

HOW IT'S DONE

Print a black and white photo of your colleague, making it semi-transparent to look like a ghost. Cut out their head and make 20-100 copies. Mix these "ghost" copies into the copier's paper feed. As people use the copier, they'll begin to notice the eerie addition of your colleague's ghost-like figure on their documents.

PRANK EXECUTED?

Date: _____   Victim: _____

HOW DID IT GO?

Repeat Worthy?

#27 THE SLIPPERY DOORKNOB

WHAT YOU'LL NEED

Vaseline or petroleum jelly

HOW IT'S DONE

Apply a thin layer of Vaseline or petroleum jelly to the doorknob of a frequently used door, such as the bathroom or break room door. The goal is to coat the doorknob just enough to make it slippery without being overly messy. Once you've set up the prank, stay nearby to observe the reactions of unsuspecting coworkers as they encounter the slick doorknob, resulting in moments of confusion.

PRANK EXECUTED?

Date: Victim:

HOW DID IT GO?

Repeat Worthy? 👍👎

#28 THE PERSISTENT PENNY PLOY

WHAT YOU'LL NEED

A handful of pennies, stealth.

HOW IT'S DONE

Begin by discreetly placing a single penny in a specific spot on your coworker's desk when they're not looking. Continue this action every few days, gradually adding more pennies to the same location. The aim is to slowly escalate their confusion and curiosity without immediately revealing the prank. As the number of pennies increases, so will their wonderment about where these coins are coming from.

PRANK EXECUTED?

Date: Victim:

HOW DID IT GO?

Repeat Worthy?

#29 ARACHNID IN THE ATTIC

WHAT YOU'LL NEED

A black marker, a roll of toilet paper.

HOW IT'S DONE

Draw a realistic-looking spider on the first few sheets of the toilet paper roll. Aim for a spot that will be immediately visible when the next person goes to use the paper. Carefully place the roll back on its holder with the spider drawing poised for the best effect. The unsuspecting individual reaching for the paper will be met with a surprise scare.

PRANK EXECUTED?

Date: _____ Victim: _____

HOW DID IT GO?

Repeat Worthy? 👍👎

#30 GOOGLY-EYED GALLERY

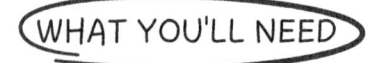

WHAT YOU'LL NEED

Googly eyes, adhesive, access to a coworker's framed photos.

HOW IT'S DONE

Spice up your colleague's desk decor by adding a pair of googly eyes to their treasured framed pictures. Carefully place the eyes over faces in the photos for a startlingly funny transformation. The true amusement lies in the subtlety of the switch: how long will it take them to spot the goofy gaze of their "loved ones"?

PRANK EXECUTED?

Date: .... Victim: ....

HOW DID IT GO? 😊 😐 😠

Repeat Worthy? 👍👎

#31 THE COFFEE BLOCK

WHAT YOU'LL NEED

Coffee maker, freezer.

HOW IT'S DONE

This chilly ruse is perfect for the java-loving office. Brew a pot of coffee at the end of the day, then stealthily stash it in the freezer. The next morning, return the solid coffee block to its rightful place. Watch as caffeine-seekers try to pour their morning cup, only to find their beloved brew is an impenetrable ice block. Just be ready with a fresh pot to thaw any frosty feelings!

PRANK EXECUTED?

Date: _____ Victim: _____

HOW DID IT GO?

Repeat Worthy?

#32 GHOST MOUSE MAYHEM

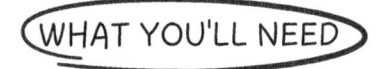

WHAT YOU'LL NEED

A wireless mouse, a coworker's computer with USB access

HOW IT'S DONE

Create a tech poltergeist by secretly plugging a wireless mouse receiver into your colleague's computer. Then, from a safe distance, give the mouse a nudge every now and then. They'll be baffled as their cursor dances across the screen with a mind of its own. Just a few clicks here and there will lead to a comical confusion. Keep the mystery alive as long as you can before revealing the trick behind the tech!

PRANK EXECUTED?

Date: _____   Victim: _____

HOW DID IT GO? 😊 😐 😠

Repeat Worthy? 👍 👎

#33 THE FAKE POO

WHAT YOU'LL NEED

A bar of chocolate, nuts or cereal for texture.

HOW IT'S DONE

Melt a bar of chocolate and mix it with nuts or cereal to give it that realistic texture. Mold it into the dreaded shape and strategically place your creation in places like on top of a toilet seat, under a desk, on the floor... It's crude, it's sure to evoke a reaction, and it's absolutely hilarious. Watch and wait for the shrieks and then the laughter when they realize it's just a harmless, albeit cheeky, chocolate concoction.

PRANK EXECUTED?

Date: _____ Victim: _____

HOW DID IT GO? 😊 😐 😠

_____
_____
_____
_____

Repeat Worthy? 👍👎

#34 THE WRAP TRAP

WHAT YOU'LL NEED

Several rolls of plastic wrap

HOW IT'S DONE

Wait for your colleague to step away, then get to work encasing their desk, chair, and all their office supplies in plastic wrap. Layer it on thick for maximum effect. It's a prank that's as clear as it is clingy, and it'll require some patience to unwrap the day's tasks. Just stand back and watch the unwrapping ceremony begin!

PRANK EXECUTED?

Date: _____ Victim: _____

HOW DID IT GO?

_____
_____
_____
_____

Repeat Worthy? 👍👎

#35 THE "OUT OF ORDER" MIRROR

WHAT YOU'LL NEED

Paper, printer or marker.

HOW IT'S DONE

Create confusion with a simple sign that reads "Mirror under repair. Please do not use," and place it on a perfectly functional mirror. Watch as people stop to puzzle over the idea of a mirror being 'out of service'. Are their reflections under maintenance too? It's the perfect mix-up for double-takes and chuckles in the bathroom or hallway.

PRANK EXECUTED?

Date: _____ Victim: _____

HOW DID IT GO?

Repeat Worthy?

#36 CREAMY SURPRISE

WHAT YOU'LL NEED

Cream-filled cookies, toothpaste.

HOW IT'S DONE

Carefully open the cookies and scrape out the original cream. Replace it with toothpaste and reassemble the cookies. Offer them to your friends, anticipating their surprise at the unexpected minty flavor instead of the sweet cream they were expecting. Just be in on the joke and ready with some real cookies to share afterwards, turning the prank into a shared moment of fun and laughter.

PRANK EXECUTED?

Date: _____ Victim: _____

HOW DID IT GO? 😊 😐 😠

_____
_____
_____
_____

Repeat Worthy? 👍 👎

#37 THE LATHERLESS SOAP

WHAT YOU'LL NEED

A bar of soap, clear nail polish.

HOW IT'S DONE

Apply a layer of clear nail polish all over the bar of soap. Put it back in the workplace bathroom and watch as coworkers struggle to get it to lather, leading to confusion and laughter. Be sure to have an untreated bar of soap on hand for those who prefer to opt out of the prank and simply wash their hands.

PRANK EXECUTED?

Date: Victim:

HOW DID IT GO?

Repeat Worthy?

#38 DESK DRAWER CRITTERS

WHAT YOU'LL NEED

Rubber snakes or arachnids.

HOW IT'S DONE

Sneak a few rubber snakes or arachnids into the desk drawer of a coworker who's not fond of insects. Hide them beneath papers or office supplies for an added surprise element. Anticipate their startled discovery and share a good-natured laugh as they uncover the playful ruse.

PRANK EXECUTED?

Date: _____ Victim: _____

HOW DID IT GO?

Repeat Worthy?

#39 THE MYSTERY MOVE-IN

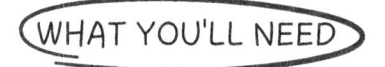

WHAT YOU'LL NEED

Taped and sealed moving boxes.

HOW IT'S DONE

Fill a coworker's cubicle or office with taped and sealed boxes, creating the illusion of an impending office move or a new roommate. The setup aims to spark curiosity and mild confusion as they ponder the origins and intentions behind the unexpected delivery. Watch as they try to decode the situation, leading to a mix of speculation and anticipation.

PRANK EXECUTED?

Date: Victim:

HOW DID IT GO?

Repeat Worthy? 👍👎

#40 THE UNBIRTHDAY SURPRISE

WHAT YOU'LL NEED

Balloons, Cake, Birthday cards (signed by coworkers)

HOW IT'S DONE

Decorate a teammate's workspace with balloons and place a cake nearby, accompanied by birthday cards signed by all the coworkers. As the final touch, initiate a round of "Happy Birthday" singing. The catch? It's not actually their birthday. This prank thrives on the element of surprise and confusion, as the person tries to understand why their "birthday" is being celebrated on a completely arbitrary day.

PRANK EXECUTED?

Date: _____   Victim: _____

HOW DID IT GO?   😊 😐 😠

_____
_____
_____

Repeat Worthy? 👍👎

40

#41 THE TYPIST'S TWISTER

WHAT YOU'LL NEED

A keyboard with removable keys.

HOW IT'S DONE

Carefully exchange the M and N keys, along with a few other pairs like S and D, or A and E, on a coworker's keyboard. This clever rearrangement creates a challenging puzzle for your colleague as they try to type. Inform the IT department beforehand to ensure they're ready for any confused requests for help.

PRANK EXECUTED?

Date: Victim:

HOW DID IT GO?

Repeat Worthy?

#42 THE PHANTOM MEOW

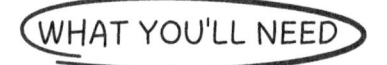

WHAT YOU'LL NEED

A small Bluetooth speaker, a recording of a cat meowing.

HOW IT'S DONE

Hide the Bluetooth speaker in a discreet location near your coworker's workspace. Every few minutes, play the cat meowing sound. The sporadic meows will spark curiosity and a mini hunt for the non-existent cat.

PRANK EXECUTED?

Date: .... Victim: ....

HOW DID IT GO?

Repeat Worthy?

#43 THE MYSTERIOUS MEMO MIX-UP

WHAT YOU'LL NEED

Post-It notes, a pen.

HOW IT'S DONE

Stick Post-Its around a coworker's desk with amusing, out-of-the-ordinary tasks or messages they didn't write. Suggestions like "buy birdseed" for someone without a bird, or notes about imaginary meetings such as "Urgent! Meeting in the conference room at 1 p.m." can create a delightful puzzle. Add a note saying "Come see me," without specifying who it's from, to add to the intrigue.

PRANK EXECUTED?

Date: _____ Victim: _____

HOW DID IT GO?

Repeat Worthy?

43

#44 THE COPYCAT PAPERCLIP

WHAT YOU'LL NEED

A paperclip, access to a copier.

HOW IT'S DONE

Place a paperclip on the copier's glass in the top left corner and make several copies. Swap the copier's blank paper with these paperclip-marked copies. As coworkers print their documents, they'll be puzzled by the mysterious paperclip appearing on every page.

PRANK EXECUTED?

Date: _____   Victim: _____

HOW DID IT GO?

Repeat Worthy?

#45 THE SCENTED SEAT

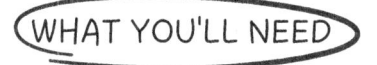

WHAT YOU'LL NEED

Car air freshener trees, tape.

HOW IT'S DONE

Secretly tape a few car air freshener trees under your coworker's office chair. As the scent slowly fills their space, watch their puzzled reactions as they try to pinpoint the source of the unexpected fragrance.

PRANK EXECUTED?

Date: Victim:

HOW DID IT GO?

Repeat Worthy? 👍👎

#46 THE PHANTOM PRINTOUT PUZZLE

WHAT YOU'LL NEED

Access to a shared printer.

HOW IT'S DONE

Wait until a coworker sends a document to the printer. Secretly queue up an extra 10 or more blank pages to print right after their job. As they collect their printout, their confusion over the unexpected blank pages adds a touch of mystery and amusement.

PRANK EXECUTED?

Date: _____ Victim: _____

HOW DID IT GO?

Repeat Worthy? 👍👎

#47 THE GREAT COFFEE HUNT

WHAT YOU'LL NEED

Access to the office coffee supplies.

HOW IT'S DONE

Temporarily relocate the coffee machine to an unconventional spot, such as under the sink or tucked away in the fridge's back. Bring your personal coffee supply for the day and observe as your colleagues embark on a caffeine quest first thing in the morning.

PRANK EXECUTED?

Date: Victim:

HOW DID IT GO?

Repeat Worthy?

#48 I SEE YOU

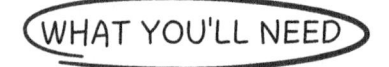

WHAT YOU'LL NEED

Sticky googly eyes.

HOW IT'S DONE

Get to the office early and attach a pair of sticky googly eyes to every item inside the office refrigerator. Make sure every piece of food, drink container, and even the shelves themselves have eyes. When coworkers go to open the fridge, they'll find a surprising scene: every item seemingly "alive" and staring back at them.

PRANK EXECUTED?

Date: _____ Victim: _____

HOW DID IT GO?

Repeat Worthy?

#49 THE PARKING PLOT

WHAT YOU'LL NEED

Access to a coworker's car keys, A nearby parking lot

HOW IT'S DONE

Sneakily borrow a coworker's car keys and relocate their vehicle to a different parking lot. Witness the bewildered search party form as they hunt for their missing ride. After they've had a moment to experience the mild panic of a "missing" vehicle, step in and play the prankster's guide, leading them to the unexpectedly relocated car.

PRANK EXECUTED?

Date: .... Victim: ....

HOW DID IT GO?

_____
_____
_____
_____

Repeat Worthy? 👍👎

#50 THE FAUXSTING BOX

WHAT YOU'LL NEED

A cardboard box, frosting or whipped cream

HOW IT'S DONE

Transform a cardboard box into a faux cake by adding frosting or whipped cream on top. Place it in the break room with a sign saying "Please Help Yourself" and include a plastic knife nearby. Watch as curious colleagues attempt to slice into the "cake," only to be met with confusion and laughter when they realize it's just a deliciously deceptive prank. It's a sweet joke without the calories!

PRANK EXECUTED?

Date: _____ Victim: _____

HOW DID IT GO?

Repeat Worthy?

#51 OFFICE CRIME SCENE

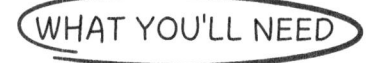

WHAT YOU'LL NEED

Fake crime scene tape, Chalk or washable marker

HOW IT'S DONE

Use the fake crime scene tape to section off an area in a common space of the office. With chalk or a washable marker, draw an outline of a 'body' on the floor within the cordoned area. When colleagues arrive, they'll step into a lighthearted "investigation." Watch the giggles unfold as they guess 'whodunit'!

PRANK EXECUTED?

Date: Victim:

HOW DID IT GO?

Repeat Worthy?

51

#52 THE GHOST DESKTOP

WHAT YOU'LL NEED

Access to your coworker's computer

HOW IT'S DONE

Grab a chance when your coworker is away to snap a screenshot of their desktop. Then, move all their icons into a new folder and stash it in their documents. Set the screenshot as their desktop background. Now, wait for the moment of confusion as they click away at their unresponsive "icons."

PRANK EXECUTED?

Date: Victim:

HOW DID IT GO?

Repeat Worthy?

#53 THE SCRATCH SCARE

WHAT YOU'LL NEED

A notepad, a pen

HOW IT'S DONE

Write a sincere apology note claiming you accidentally scratched their car and place it on their windshield. The anticipation builds as your colleague examines every inch of their vehicle, searching for a non-existent scratch. Watch from a distance as the search turns into puzzled relief!

PRANK EXECUTED?

Date: Victim:

HOW DID IT GO?

Repeat Worthy?

#54 THE CHATTY COPIER

WHAT YOU'LL NEED

A sticky note, a pen

HOW IT'S DONE

Write a note stating that the office copier has been upgraded to include voice activation feature. Affix this note prominently on the copier. Position yourself where you can observe the reactions without being too conspicuous. As colleagues approach and read the note, they'll likely attempt to use the voice commands, speaking to the copier in hopes of triggering a response.

PRANK EXECUTED?

Date: _____ Victim: _____

HOW DID IT GO?

Repeat Worthy?

#55 THE BOTTOMLESS BOX

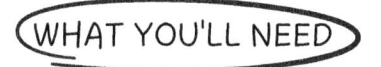

WHAT YOU'LL NEED

A medium-sized cardboard box, a cutter or scissors.

HOW IT'S DONE

Carefully cut out the bottom of a cardboard box. Place it on your coworker's desk and fill it with lightweight office supplies. Watch in amusement as they attempt to lift the box, only to find the contents spilling out from the bottom.

PRANK EXECUTED?

Date: Victim:

HOW DID IT GO?

Repeat Worthy?

#56 THE NEVER-ENDING DOCUMENT

WHAT YOU'LL NEED

Access to a coworker's digital documents, a very long and repetitive text file.

HOW IT'S DONE

Infiltrate your coworker's document and discreetly add hundreds of pages of lorem ipsum or repetitive text to the end. As they innocently scroll down, they'll be met with a seemingly endless document, leaving them baffled and amused by the unexpected prank. Just sit back and enjoy their priceless reaction to the infinite scroll!

PRANK EXECUTED?

Date: _____　Victim: _____

HOW DID IT GO?

Repeat Worthy? 👍👎

#57 THE UN-CLOSABLE DOOR

WHAT YOU'LL NEED

A small object to obstruct the door mechanism, tape.

HOW IT'S DONE

Secretly tape a small object onto the door latch of a commonly used door, preventing it from latching closed. Watch as people keep trying to shut it, only to find it swings back open. It's a harmless way to confuse everyone and keep things open!

PRANK EXECUTED?

Date:　　　　　　　Victim:

HOW DID IT GO?

Repeat Worthy? 👍👎

#58 THE FRIDGE FRIGHT

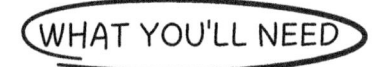

WHAT YOU'LL NEED

A laminated photo of a face, a large jar, office fridge.

HOW IT'S DONE

Print a life-sized photo of a face, ensuring it's detailed and eerie. Laminate it for water resistance and place it in a large clear jar filled with water tinted green. Carefully hide the jar in the office fridge amidst the lunch items. When someone innocently opens the fridge, they'll be met with a chilling surprise as the face stares back at them from the murky depths.

PRANK EXECUTED?

Date: Victim:

HOW DID IT GO?

Repeat Worthy?

#59 THE LABEL EVERYTHING

WHAT YOU'LL NEED

A label maker, your coworker's desk and belongings.

HOW IT'S DONE

Use a label maker to Tag every single item, from pens to post-its, and even the desk itself with hilariously detailed labels. Get creative with the labels, employing humorously detailed descriptions that go beyond mere identification. The over-the-top organization will give them a laugh when they see their 'newly categorized' workspace.

PRANK EXECUTED?

Date: Victim:

HOW DID IT GO?

Repeat Worthy?

#60 THE SHATTERED SCREEN

WHAT YOU'LL NEED

A wallpaper or screensaver of a cracked screen.

HOW IT'S DONE

Stealthily access your coworker's computer and change their wallpaper to a realistic image of a shattered screen. When they return to their desk, they'll be in for a shock, thinking their monitor is broken. Enjoy the moment of confusion and laughter as they realize it's just a harmless prank, and their screen is intact!

PRANK EXECUTED?

Date: Victim:

HOW DID IT GO?

Repeat Worthy?

#61 THE ERRATIC MOUSE

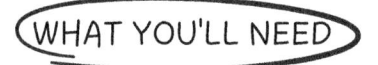

WHAT YOU'LL NEED

Access to your coworker's mouse settings.

HOW IT'S DONE

Go into the mouse settings on your coworker's computer and max out the speed, or if possible, change the direction of the mouse movement. They'll be puzzled by their suddenly uncontrollable cursor.

PRANK EXECUTED?

Date: .... Victim: ....

HOW DID IT GO?

Repeat Worthy?

#62 MUGSHOT SURPRISES

WHAT YOU'LL NEED

Sticky notes or tape, Pen or marker

HOW IT'S DONE

After everyone has left work, quietly make your way to the mug cabinet. Use sticky notes or tape to attach witty messages or drawings to the bottom of each mug. These hidden messages stay concealed from the person using the mug but promise a visual surprise for anyone else when the mug is raised. Carefully place the mugs back, ensuring the notes are secure but unseen.

PRANK EXECUTED?

Date: Victim:

HOW DID IT GO?

Repeat Worthy?

#63 CASH HUNT CLIFFHANGER

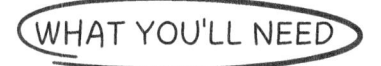

WHAT YOU'LL NEED

Dollar bill, Scissors, Sticky notes, Pen

HOW IT'S DONE

Slice a dollar into quarters, then secure each to a sticky note. Hide them under office essentials—only the dollar part peeks out. The twist? A note that quips, "Congrats! You're a quarter richer... in experience!" Cue the office-wide treasure hunt with a side of chuckles.. The twist? A note that quips, "Congrats! You're a quarter richer... in experience!" Cue the office-wide treasure hunt with a side of chuckles.

PRANK EXECUTED?

Date: _____ Victim: _____

HOW DID IT GO? 😊 😐 😠

_____
_____
_____
_____

Repeat Worthy? 👍 👎

#64 SCENT OF SURPRISE

WHAT YOU'LL NEED

Odd-smelling cologne, Febreze bottle label, Adhesive

HOW IT'S DONE

Obtain a cologne with a unique or strong scent and secure a Febreze bottle label around it using adhesive. Subtly spritz this concoction in communal office areas. As the aroma permeates, watch as the office reacts to the unconventional scent, with reactions ranging from curiosity to amusement.

PRANK EXECUTED?

Date: Victim:

HOW DID IT GO?

Repeat Worthy?

#65 THE UNSLICEABLE SURPRISE

WHAT YOU'LL NEED

Large sponge, Icing, Sprinkles, Cake knife

HOW IT'S DONE

Cover a car wash sponge thoroughly with icing, decorating it with sprinkles to resemble a delicious cake. Place this convincing confection in a common area, complete with a cake knife for the "cutting ceremony." As someone attempts to slice into this faux dessert, the realization that it's actually an unsliceable sponge will dawn, turning anticipation into a wave of laughter.

PRANK EXECUTED?

Date: Victim:

HOW DID IT GO?

Repeat Worthy? 👍👎

#66 THE DESKTOP MIRAGE

WHAT YOU'LL NEED

Screenshot capability, Ability to right-click, Stealth

HOW IT'S DONE

Secretly take a screenshot of your coworker's desktop while they're away. Set this image as the desktop background. Next, hide all desktop icons. When your coworker returns, they'll be baffled, clicking on the non-responsive icons that are merely part of the background image.

PRANK EXECUTED?

Date: _____ Victim: _____

HOW DID IT GO?

Repeat Worthy?

#67 THE ENDLESS UPDATE

WHAT YOU'LL NEED

Access to coworker's PC, Internet, Slyness

HOW IT'S DONE

Go to fakeupdate.net and select an update screen that matches your colleague's operating system. Set the browser to fullscreen mode to conceal any giveaways of the prank, then discreetly leave the scene. Watch from afar as your colleague returns, puzzled by the update's seemingly endless cycle of progress and regression, culminating in a humorous fake error message.

PRANK EXECUTED?

Date: _____   Victim: _____

HOW DID IT GO? 😊 😐 😠

_____
_____
_____
_____

Repeat Worthy? 👍 👎

#68 THE TEMPTATION TEST

WHAT YOU'LL NEED

Treats (cookies, brownies, cake),
Label for food "DO NOT EAT" or "For X'S Birthday"

HOW IT'S DONE

Purchase and leave some treats, like a birthday cake, in the breakroom. Label it with 'DO NOT EAT' or 'For [Name]'s Birthday.' When someone enters the kitchen, start eating it and observe their reaction. Then, with a sly grin, offer them a piece. Witness the whirl of their moral compass!

PRANK EXECUTED?

Date: _____ Victim: _____

HOW DID IT GO? 😊 😐 😠

_____
_____
_____
_____

Repeat Worthy? 👍 👎

#69 THE GREAT SWEET SWAP

WHAT YOU'LL NEED

Sugar and salt packets

HOW IT'S DONE

Sneak into the kitchen and swap the sugar with salt. Place salt where sugar usually is, next to the coffee, and sugar where salt goes, by the pepper. Wait and watch as the morning coffee routine turns into a taste bud adventure. How long until the mix-up is noticed?

PRANK EXECUTED?

Date: _____ Victim: _____

HOW DID IT GO?

Repeat Worthy?

#70 STAPLER HOSTAGE HEIST

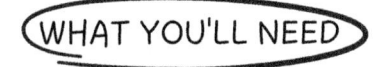

WHAT YOU'LL NEED

A borrowed stapler from a coworker,
Paper and pen for your quirky ransom note

HOW IT'S DONE

Secretly take a stapler from a coworker's desk and leave behind a playful ransom note. The note should demand an amusing payment, like a pile of paper clips or an office-wide email featuring "Party in the USA" lyrics, for the stapler's return.

PRANK EXECUTED?

Date: _____ Victim: _____

HOW DID IT GO?

Repeat Worthy? 👍👎

#71 THE OUTLANDISH CLIENT REQUEST

WHAT YOU'LL NEED

A phone or email access, A knack for theatrics

HOW IT'S DONE

Pose as a client and contact a coworker, demanding services that are hilariously beyond the scope of your company. Whether it's asking for a moon rock delivery or a time travel tour package, the more absurd, the better. Enjoy the bewildered reactions as your coworker tries to navigate your preposterous request.

PRANK EXECUTED?

Date: _____ Victim: _____

HOW DID IT GO?

_____
_____
_____
_____

Repeat Worthy? 👍 👎

#72 EXECUTIVE FACE SWAP

WHAT YOU'LL NEED

One photo of your boss's face, A printer, Scissors, Tape

HOW IT'S DONE

Choose an iconic photo of your boss and print it in various sizes to match your coworker's picture frame dimensions. Stealthily cut out the boss's face from these prints and apply them over the faces in the frames on your coworker's desk. The unsuspecting discovery that their personal photos now feature the boss will spark immediate laughter and double takes around the office.

PRANK EXECUTED?

Date: .... Victim: ....

HOW DID IT GO? 😊 😐 😠

Repeat Worthy? 👍 👎

#73 THE SILENT TECH TANGO

WHAT YOU'LL NEED

Access to a coworker's computer

HOW IT'S DONE

Quietly unplug the keyboard or mouse from a colleague's computer. For an extra twist, activate the voice-reader feature. Watch as they puzzle over the sudden narration of their screen, compounded by their unresponsive peripherals.

PRANK EXECUTED?

Date: Victim:

HOW DID IT GO?

Repeat Worthy?

#74 THE UNQUENCHABLE THIRST

WHAT YOU'LL NEED

Bottled beverages, Superglue

HOW IT'S DONE

First, buy some bottled sodas, waters, or any other beverages suitable for work. Then, secretly superglue the lids shut and place them with a note encouraging your coworkers to grab a free drink. Enjoy their expressions of surprise and mock despair when they can't open them. Be ready with a genuine offer to replace the glued bottles with drinkable ones.

PRANK EXECUTED?

Date: Victim:

HOW DID IT GO?

Repeat Worthy?

#75 THE CHATTY FLORA

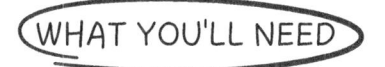

WHAT YOU'LL NEED

Walkie-talkie

HOW IT'S DONE

Conceal a walkie-talkie inside a plant. Occasionally, broadcast comments, tasks, or compliments, making it seem as though the plant is speaking. The more bizarre or humorous, the better, especially if your device can alter your voice. Witness the office's bemusement and delight as they try to decode the source of this botanical banter.

PRANK EXECUTED?

Date: _____ Victim: _____

HOW DID IT GO?

_____
_____
_____
_____

Repeat Worthy? 👍👎

#76 FROZEN BUGS

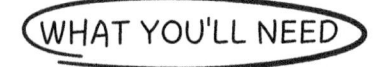

WHAT YOU'LL NEED

Plastic bugs, Ice cube tray

HOW IT'S DONE

Freeze plastic bugs in ice cubes and sneak them into an iced drink for a coworker. Whether you mix it at work or grab it from a coffee shop, make sure your special cubes are part of the chill. Offer the bug-infused beverage with a smile, and wait for the moment of discovery. The initial sip might be refreshing, but the realization will bring a mix of shock and laughter, making for an unforgettable drink.

PRANK EXECUTED?

Date: _____ Victim: _____

HOW DID IT GO? 😊 😕 😠

_____
_____
_____
_____

Repeat Worthy? 👍 👎

#77 THE DESK DILEMMA

WHAT YOU'LL NEED

"For Sale" or "Now Hiring" sign

HOW IT'S DONE

Secure a "For Sale" or "Now Hiring" sign and position it noticeably on a coworker's desk during a moment they're absent. The sudden presence of such a sign will spark a blend of confusion and curiosity among everyone who sees it, including the desk's owner and potentially the boss.

PRANK EXECUTED?

Date: _____ Victim: _____

HOW DID IT GO?

Repeat Worthy? 👍👎

#78 THE BACKWARD BUREAU

WHAT YOU'LL NEED

A coworker's desk and its contents

HOW IT'S DONE

Flip everything at your coworker's desk to face the opposite direction: monitor to the wall, keyboard turned away, and even the chair on the wrong side. If you can, reorient the desk, printer, and other movable items too.

PRANK EXECUTED?

Date: .... Victim: ....

HOW DID IT GO? 😊 😐 😠

Repeat Worthy? 👍 👎

#79 THE UNWRAPPING URGE

WHAT YOU'LL NEED

Gift wrapping paper, Boxes of various sizes

HOW IT'S DONE

Wrap boxes within boxes, each layer revealing another until the smallest one is found. Inside, place a sticky note with "Get back to work!" on it. Gift it to your coworker as a token for their hard work, watching their anticipation grow with each layer.

PRANK EXECUTED?

Date: .... Victim: ....

HOW DID IT GO?

Repeat Worthy? 👍👎

#80 SOLO COSTUME DAY

WHAT YOU'LL NEED

Access to email

HOW IT'S DONE

Send a special "office-wide" email to your chosen coworker, declaring a fictional costume day. Encourage them to arrive dressed as a fairy tale princess, a superhero, or a wall-crawling hero, making sure you're the only one in on the joke. When they step into the office decked out in a unique outfit amidst standard business attire, the scene will be priceless.

PRANK EXECUTED?

Date: Victim:

HOW DID IT GO?

Repeat Worthy?

#81 THE NEVER-RIGHT CHAIR

WHAT YOU'LL NEED

Stealth, Timing

HOW IT'S DONE

Sneak over to your colleague's desk whenever they step away and give their chair a slight adjustment: lower it a bit each time. Watch as they return, puzzled and adjusting, day after day, never catching on to the gentle prankster at work. A slow game, but the confusion is priceless.

PRANK EXECUTED?

Date: _____ Victim: _____

HOW DID IT GO?

_____
_____
_____
_____

Repeat Worthy? 👍👎

#82 THE PHANTOM BROADCAST

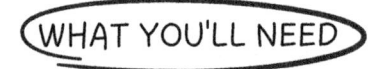

WHAT YOU'LL NEED

A small radio, Access to the ceiling tiles

HOW IT'S DONE

Slip a tiny radio above your colleague's desk, hidden within the ceiling. Tune it to an annoying station, volume just above a whisper. Deny hearing anything when they ask, sparking a mix of confusion and self-doubt. "Noise? What noise? Are you sure you're alright?" Watch the bewildered expressions multiply with every phantom sound wave.

PRANK EXECUTED?

Date: Victim:

HOW DID IT GO?

Repeat Worthy?

#83 THE CHAMELEON COUTURE

WHAT YOU'LL NEED

A collection of distinct outfits

HOW IT'S DONE

Transform your workday into a runway by swapping outfits every half hour. Ensure the same colleagues catch each fashion debut. Confused glances? Respond with a puzzled, "Whatever do you mean?" Elevate the game with each wardrobe switch, leaving witnesses to question their own perception—or your collection of clones.

PRANK EXECUTED?

Date: _____   Victim: _____

HOW DID IT GO? 😊 😐 😠

_____
_____
_____
_____

Repeat Worthy? 👍 👎

#84 THE WAITING GAME

WHAT YOU'LL NEED

Sticky notes, A knack for suspense

HOW IT'S DONE

Start the day by spreading rumors of an epic prank. Leave vague, mysterious notes around saying "Be prepared," or "Today's the day." Throughout the day, give your target those sneaky glances and sly smirks, making them expect something big. But here's the catch: do absolutely nothing. At day's end, reveal the truth with a grin, "The greatest prank was no prank at all."

PRANK EXECUTED?

Date: Victim:

HOW DID IT GO?

Repeat Worthy?

#85 THE GREAT VANISHING DISPLAY

WHAT YOU'LL NEED

Access to your coworker's computer

HOW IT'S DONE

Wait for the perfect moment when your coworker steps away from their desk. Quickly, and oh so sneakily, dive into their display settings and dial both the brightness and contrast down to zero. When they return, they'll find their screen as dark as a moonless night. Watch from a distance as they ponder the mystery of their invisible desktop.

PRANK EXECUTED?

Date: .... Victim: ....

HOW DID IT GO?

Repeat Worthy?

#86 THE SILENT SPEAKER

WHAT YOU'LL NEED

A picture of the phone's receiver, Tape matching the phone's color, A black marker

HOW IT'S DONE

Snap a photo of your coworker's phone receiver for color matching. Find tape at an office supply store that's a perfect match. When your coworker steps out, apply the tape carefully over the mouthpiece, ensuring it doesn't wrap around and give away the prank. Use the marker to mimic this pattern on the tape. This detailed touch is key to keeping the tape undetected.

PRANK EXECUTED?

Date: _____ Victim: _____

HOW DID IT GO?

Repeat Worthy?

#87 THE SEAT SYMPHONY

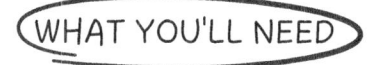

WHAT YOU'LL NEED

A whoopee cushion

HOW IT'S DONE

First, inflate the whoopee cushion enough so that it'll make noise, but not too much that it looks obvious. Find a coworker who uses an extra cushion or hangs their sweater on their chair. Secretly place the whoopee cushion under their seat cushion or behind their backrest, then cover it with their sweater to keep it hidden. Wait for them to sit down for an unexpected musical chair moment.

PRANK EXECUTED?

Date: _____ Victim: _____

HOW DID IT GO?

_____
_____
_____
_____

Repeat Worthy? 👍 👎

#88 THE OFFICE GAZETTE

WHAT YOU'LL NEED

Access to a newspaper template online

HOW IT'S DONE

Create a fake "The Office Gazette: Special Edition" using an online service, styled like a local paper with absurd yet amusing headlines, like "Office Wins Lottery: Work Optional Next Monday!" Include articles and photos for authenticity. Once ready, email it to everyone in the office or have it printed up and leave it in the office.

PRANK EXECUTED?

Date: Victim:

HOW DID IT GO?

Repeat Worthy?

#89 THE FAUX MILK MISHAP

WHAT YOU'LL NEED

White glue, A glass surface, A little soap

HOW IT'S DONE

Spread white glue on a glass surface, shaping it to look like spilled milk. Lightly soap the glass first to ensure the glue creation can be easily lifted off after drying. Leave it overnight to set. The next day, carefully place the dried glue "spill" on your friend's laptop. Watch as they gasp at the sight, only to discover the harmless, laughter-inducing truth.

PRANK EXECUTED?

Date: Victim:

HOW DID IT GO?

Repeat Worthy?

#90 THE UNEXPECTED WORKDAY

WHAT YOU'LL NEED

A cooperative friend in HR

HOW IT'S DONE

Team up with your HR buddy to craft an official-looking email that informs your friends they're required at the office the next day, despite it being a weekend. The key is in the details: make it believable but not too alarming. Send it out and then sit back to enjoy the range of reactions, from disbelief to mock outrage, before revealing the jest.

PRANK EXECUTED?

Date: Victim:

HOW DID IT GO?

Repeat Worthy?

#91 THE FAUX PARKING TICKET

WHAT YOU'LL NEED

Printer, paper, adhesive

HOW IT'S DONE

First, whip up a parking ticket using your friend's vehicle information. the fine amount listed should be absurdly high, akin to the cost of illicitly parking on the moon. Next, stick it onto their windshield in a spot they can't miss. Hide nearby and watch the drama unfold.

PRANK EXECUTED?

Date: Victim:

HOW DID IT GO?

Repeat Worthy?

#92 THE WILD CALL

WHAT YOU'LL NEED

Pen, notepad, access to your boss's desk, local zoo's phone number.

HOW IT'S DONE

Secretly leave a note on your boss's desk, pretending it's from a Mr. Bear seeking a partnership lunch. Use the zoo's number as his contact. When your boss eagerly dials, expecting a business chat, and instead gets the zoo, the confusion will be priceless. If they proceed to inquire about speaking with Mr. Bear.

PRANK EXECUTED?

Date: Victim:

HOW DID IT GO?

Repeat Worthy?

#93 THE RESTROOM RUSE

WHAT YOU'LL NEED

Paper, marker, tape, a flair for the dramatic.

HOW IT'S DONE

Stealthily place "Out of Order" signs on every bathroom door throughout the office. Watch the confusion and temporary dismay unfold as coworkers wonder about their next steps. Right when the puzzle seems unsolvable, reveal the playful deception.

PRANK EXECUTED?

Date: _____   Victim: _____

HOW DID IT GO? 😊 😐 😠

Repeat Worthy? 👍 👎

#94 THE BOSS'S NUMBER

WHAT YOU'LL NEED

Your friend's phone

HOW IT'S DONE

Grab your buddy's phone when they're not looking and change your number in it to their boss's number. Then, start sending them funny and crazy text messages pretending to be the boss. Watch them freak out and try to figure out what's going on. When you see they've had enough, let them in on the joke.

PRANK EXECUTED?

Date: _____ Victim: _____

HOW DID IT GO?

Repeat Worthy? 👍👎

#95 THE WATCHFUL EYE

WHAT YOU'LL NEED

Fake security camera, double-sided tape, printed notice.

HOW IT'S DONE

Attach a fake security camera above the urinal in the men's bathroom. Make it look as real as possible. Beneath it, place a printed notice stating, "For Security Purposes Only - All Recordings Are Monitored." Watch as your colleagues or employees get nervous, wondering if "Big Boss" is really watching.

PRANK EXECUTED?

Date: _____ Victim: _____

HOW DID IT GO?

Repeat Worthy?

#96 THE TIE-DOWN

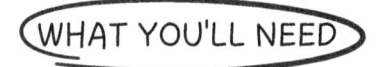

WHAT YOU'LL NEED

Strong stapler, staple remover (for a quick release).

HOW IT'S DONE

When your coworker indulges in his routine lunch break nap, skillfully staple the end of his tie to the desk, ensuring it's secure yet not damaging the fabric. Upon his awakening—naturally, without any startling slaps—witness his bewildered discovery that he finds himself unexpectedly attached to his workspace.

PRANK EXECUTED?

Date: Victim:

HOW DID IT GO?

Repeat Worthy?

#97 THE CONFETTI SURPRISE

WHAT YOU'LL NEED

Hole punch confetti, a colleague's umbrella.

HOW IT'S DONE

Wait for a moment when a colleague's umbrella is unattended. Sneak a handful of hole punch confetti into the folds before closing it neatly. The next time they open it, they'll be showered with a whimsical confetti surprise!

PRANK EXECUTED?

Date: .... Victim: ....

HOW DID IT GO? 😊 😐 😠

Repeat Worthy? 👍👎

#98 THE INKY PHONE

WHAT YOU'LL NEED

Non-permanent marker, access to your victim's desk phone.

HOW IT'S DONE

Covertly apply a thin layer of non-permanent marker ink on the earpiece and/or mouthpiece of your victim's desk phone. Aim for a color that's hard to notice but will leave a mark, like black or blue. When they next take a call, they'll unknowingly sport an ink-stamped cheek or mouth, sparking confusion and laughter when someone points it out.

PRANK EXECUTED?

Date: _____ Victim: _____

HOW DID IT GO?

Repeat Worthy?

#99 THE INVISIBLE INK FIASCO

WHAT YOU'LL NEED

Clear nail polish.

HOW IT'S DONE

Swipe a small brush of clear nail polish over the ballpoint of your colleague's pens and the tips of their pencils. Once it dries, they'll be in for a head-scratching moment when they can't jot down a single note.

PRANK EXECUTED?

Date: Victim:

HOW DID IT GO?

Repeat Worthy?

#100 THE ELEVATOR ESCAPADE

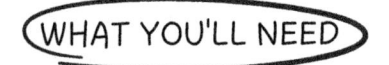

WHAT YOU'LL NEED

Paper, pen, and a strategic placement.

HOW IT'S DONE

Early in the morning, attach a convincing "Out of Service" sign on the elevator doors. Watch as your coworkers, puzzled, opt for the stairs. After they've huffed and puffed their way to the top, reveal with a grin that the elevator was in fine working order all along.

PRANK EXECUTED?

Date: Victim:

HOW DID IT GO?

Repeat Worthy?

#101 THE LEAKY CUP

WHAT YOU'LL NEED

Disposable cups, a needle.

HOW IT'S DONE

Carefully poke a few nearly invisible holes near the tops of several disposable cups at the water cooler. When your coworkers go to quench their thirst, as they tilt the cup to sip, they'll be greeted by a surprising dribble of water.

PRANK EXECUTED?

Date: .... Victim: ....

HOW DID IT GO? 😊 😐 😠

Repeat Worthy? 👍 👎

Printed in Great Britain
by Amazon